American Politics Today

The House of Representatives Today

Seth H. Pulditor

ELDORADO INK

Eldorado Ink
PO Box 100097
Pittsburgh, PA 15233
www.eldoradoink.com

Produced by OTTN Publishing, Stockton, New Jersey

CPSIA compliance information: Batch#MAP2016.
For further information, contact Eldorado Ink at info@eldoradoink.com.

First printing

1 3 5 7 9 8 6 4 2

Library of Congress Cataloging-in-Publication Data

Names: Pulditor, Seth H., author.
Title: The House of Representatives today / Seth Pulditor.
Description: Pittsburgh, PA : Eldorado Ink, [2016] | Series: American
  politics today | Includes bibliographical references and index.
Identifiers: LCCN 2016000316 | ISBN 9781619000896 (hc) | ISBN 9781619000971
  (pb) | ISBN 9781619001053 (trade) | ISBN 9781619001138 (ebook)
Subjects: LCSH: United States. Congress. House—Juvenile literature.
Classification: LCC JK1319 .P85 2016 | DDC 328.73/072—dc23
LC record available at http://lccn.loc.gov/2016000316

*For information about custom editions, special sales, or premiums,
please contact our special sales department at info@eldoradoink.com.*

Table of Contents

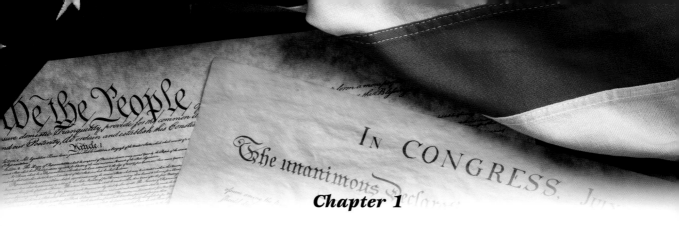

A Leadership Crisis

I n September 2015, Republican Congressman John Boehner of Ohio surprised many people by announcing that he would resign from the House of Representatives at the end of the following month. At the time Boehner was Speaker of the House, the officer who presides over the House of Representatives. This is considered one of the most important and prestigious positions in the federal government, and Boehner had held the job for nearly five years. However, by late 2015 Boehner was in a frustrating position. He had to deal not only with Democrats who opposed policies that he supported, but also with attacks from members of his own party in Congress, who were deeply divided about how to advance their party's legislative agenda.

Boehner became House Speaker after Republicans won a majority of seats in the House during the 2010 midterm elections. However, that election foreshadowed some of the challenges that Boehner

The U.S. House of Representatives is made up of 435 congressmen. They are apportioned according to population, with each member representing about 710,000 people, based on the most recent U.S. census taken in 2010. This means that the states with the most population have the most representatives. The House meets in the U.S. Capitol Building in Washington, D.C.

would face as the leader of the House. Dozens of very conservative Republicans were elected to the House of Representatives in 2010, thanks to support from so-called "Tea Party" voters who were angry about the economic and social policies of President Barack Obama's administration. The Tea Party–backed Republicans voted into the House had promised to decrease the size of the federal government and to reduce taxes. They also wanted to repeal legislation that Obama and the Democrats in Congress had passed before the midterm elec-

Liberals vs. Conservatives

When applied to the United States today, the terms *liberal* and *conservative* describe two opposing sets of political beliefs, as well as the people who hold them. Broadly speaking, liberals advocate a larger, more activist government than do conservatives.

Liberals generally favor significant government regulation of business in order to achieve goals seen to be in the public interest (for example, environmental protection, the welfare of workers, consumer protection). Conservatives believe that the less the government intervenes in economic matters, the better. Free markets, conservatives say, produce the greatest benefits for society, including maximum prosperity.

Liberals believe government must fund "safety net" programs to ensure that all citizens have a minimum standard of living. Conservatives argue that government social spending tends to breed dependency and discourage work among the groups it's intended to help. Conservatives emphasize personal responsibility as the means by which the poor should improve their lives.

Compared with liberals, conservatives tend to be less open to cultural change and more desirous of preserving "traditional values." This dynamic can be seen, for example, in the issue of same-sex marriage.

In the United States, "left" or "left-wing" is synonymous with liberal. Conservatives are known as "right-wingers" or "the right."

tion. Their primary target was the Patient Protection and Affordable Care Act, a law passed in 2009 that was intended to provide health insurance to millions of uninsured Americans.

During his career in Congress, which had begun in 1991, Boehner had always been considered conservative. He had consistently supported tax cuts and economic policies that helped businesses—core tenets of the conservative political philosophy. But a Democratic president still controlled the White House, and Boehner recognized that President Obama could veto any legislation that would roll back the Affordable Care Act. To govern the country, Boehner believed that his party would have to compromise sometimes. But pressure from the Tea Party–backed Republicans would make compromise more difficult.

SPENDING AND BORROWING

One of Congress's most important responsibilities, for example, is creating an annual spending plan called the national budget. This plan, which originates in the House of Representatives, tracks the tax revenue that the government expects to receive and allocates it to pay the costs of government programs over the course of the year. These programs include the cost of supporting the American military, providing government services, and funding social programs like Social Security and Medicare.

If the government does not collect as much in taxes as it plans to spend operating its programs, a revenue shortfall known as a deficit occurs. It has become common for federal budgets to operate with a deficit—in fact, 45 of the past 50 national budgets have called for spending more than they collected in taxes and other revenue. Deficits often total hundreds of billions of dollars each year.

To cover the deficit, the government needs to borrow money through the sale of bonds to investors from all over the world. This borrowed money becomes part of the national debt, the total amount that the U.S. government owes to creditors. It is paid back over time, with interest. Today, the federal government must borrow enough money to pay about 38 percent of the total budget each year. The national debt currently exceeds $18.4 trillion.

If Congress does not borrow enough money to pay for its programs, the government would have to shut down. Typically, any federal offices or services that are considered "non-essential" are shut down first. This can be inconvenient to many Americans, but ensures that agencies like the military are able to continue functioning as normal. Such shutdowns have occurred for short periods a few times in American history. However, if Congress cannot agree to borrow the money it needs, the entire government would eventually have to cease operations.

Congress places a limit on the total amount of money that the government is permitted to borrow from investors. This limit is known as the debt ceiling. Once it is reached, the government cannot borrow more money unless Congress agrees to make the debt ceiling higher. Historically, the debt ceiling has been increased with little fanfare. Both parties in Congress understand that they have already promised to pay for the programs in their budget, so they have no choice but to borrow money in order to fulfill their promises. Based on the rate of spending, economists can determine when the government must exceed the ceiling in order to meet its obligations.

In early 2011, experts determined that the debt ceiling would need to be raised by August of that year. If this was not done, the government would not be able to pay Social Security and Medicare benefits, the salaries of military personnel and government workers, and many other items. Failure to increase the debt ceiling before the August 2011 deadline could also have caused the federal government to default on its loan obligations to investors. This would have serious long-term consequences, because the United States has grown so dependent on borrowed money. Default would made it more difficult and expensive for the government to borrow money in the future. Investors would not buy government bonds if they did not trust that the government would live up to its promises to repay the loans when they were due.

DEBT CEILING CRISIS

In 2011 the new Republicans in the House saw the upcoming vote on the debt ceiling as an opportunity to extract some concessions on the

A 2009 Tea Party rally in Dallas opposes passage of the Patient Protection and Affordable Care Act, which was nicknamed "Obamacare" by critics. The tactics used by Democrats in Congress to pass the controversial health care legislation angered many Republicans.

budget from Democrats in Congress and the Obama administration. They refused to raise the debt ceiling unless the president agreed to spending cuts that would reduce the budget deficit. A lengthy stalemate resulted, with investors fearing a default and Americans concerned that the government would shut down.

After more than a month of negotiations, on July 31, 2011, Boehner and the Obama administration announced a deal to raise the debt ceiling in exchange for $900 million in spending reductions that would take place over a ten-year period. However, although conservatives had gotten some of what they wanted, they were not happy about the compromise. Some even said that they would have preferred to see the government shut down and default on its loan obligations.

The next time the debt ceiling needed to be raised, in 2013, conservative Republicans again refused to vote for an increase unless there were more cuts to federal spending. A group of about 40 conservative Republicans who called themselves the House Freedom Caucus refused to follow Boehner's leadership. Instead, they demanded that he allow the government to shut down in order to achieve their goals. For 16 days in October 2013, the federal government experienced a partial shutdown. About 800,000 federal employees were placed on temporary leave and were not paid. Finally, on the day that the debt was expected to exceed its ceiling, Congress voted to raise the debt ceiling again in exchange for additional spending cuts in the future.

During the government shutdown, Democrats took the opportunity to publicly blame Boehner for gridlock in Congress. They claimed that he indulged unreasonable demands from Republican hard-liners, even though these demands threatened to throw the U.S. economy into chaos. The Tea Party wing of the Republican Party, meanwhile, was unhappy with Boehner, believing he had not fought hard enough against Obama and his programs. They vowed that there would be no compromise the next time such a standoff occurred.

Because all the members of the House of Representatives are elected every two years, Congress operates in two-year sessions. Leaders must be re-elected at the start of each session. At the opening of the 114th Congress in January 2015, 25 Republicans refused to vote for Boehner. This was the most votes to oppose a sitting Speaker by members of his own party since 1923. It also meant more than twice as many Republicans strongly opposed his leadership as had at the start of the previous Congress in 2013.

The Government Accountability Office (GAO) is an independent, nonpartisan agency that works for Congress and investigates how the federal government spends taxpayer dollars. The GAO has determined that, in reaction to widespread concerns that the U.S. government would default on its debt obligations in 2013, investors charged higher interest rates on loans to the government. These resulted in the government paying about $70 million more in interest payments than expected.

President Barack Obama meets with Speaker of the House John Boehner on the patio near the Oval Office, July 3, 2011. The two leaders were discussing the debt ceiling crisis.

Another sign that Boehner's hold on the speakership was growing tenuous was a challenge led by a member of his party. In July, Representative Mark Meadows (R-NC) filed a motion to vacate the Speaker position, claiming in part that the Speaker had "used the legislative calendar to create crises for the American people, in order to compel members to vote for legislation." This sort of motion is permitted under the rules of the House, but had not been attempted in nearly a century. Meadows's motion only received modest support from other Republicans, however, and it faded away without a vote.

By the fall of 2015, as another debt-ceiling deadline loomed, Boehner recognized that he could no longer hold the Republican Party together on the issue. He announced his resignation as Speaker. At the end of October, finding a way to make the bitterly divided groups in the House of Representatives work together would become someone else's problem.

SEARCH FOR A SPEAKER

At first, it seemed that the House Majority Leader, Kevin McCarthy (R-Calif.), would become the new Speaker. This important position is chosen by a vote of all 435 members of the House of Representatives, and must receive a majority of the votes. The Republican Party held

Kevin McCarthy

247 seats in the House in 2015, compared to 188 Democratic Party seats, so the Republicans had more than the 218 votes needed to elect the next Speaker. However, members of the Freedom Caucus declared that they would not support McCarthy for Speaker because they believed his approach would be similar to that of Boehner. Without their support, McCarthy would be 10 to 15 votes short of receiving a majority.

Recognizing that he could not win the seat, McCarthy withdrew from the race. This threw the entire process into chaos. Neither the Republicans nor the Democrats could muster enough support to elect a speaker without the votes of the Freedom Caucus. The group insisted that only a candidate who was willing to shut down the government again in order to accomplish conservative goals would be acceptable to them as speaker. However, the candidates that the Freedom Caucus proposed were not acceptable to the larger group of Republicans in the House.

Republicans might have proposed a more moderate candidate in hopes of drawing enough votes from Democrats to elect a new Speaker. However, they were unwilling to do this. Such a move would have angered and alienated their conservative supporters even further. In any case, cooperation between Republicans and Democrats has become nearly unthinkable. The two parties have become so bitterly divided in their beliefs, and so antagonistic toward one another, that bipartisan cooperation has all but disappeared from Congress.

POLITICAL POLARIZATION

Political scientists have developed various methods for measuring the ideology of lawmakers. One of the most widely used, known as DW-

NOMINATE, is based on roll-call votes. It places legislators on a scale of -1.0 (most liberal) to +1.0 (most conservative). Those who score between -0.25 and 0.25 are classified as moderates. Centrist scores range up to 0.5 from zero (in either direction). Legislators whose scores fall below -0.5 or above +0.5 are deemed highly liberal or highly conservative.

DW-NOMINATE's indirect way of measuring ideology yields results that track closely with results obtained through other methods, including the legislative "scorecards" compiled by interest groups such as the liberal Americans for Democratic Action and the American Conservative Union. And this system offers political scientists an extremely useful tool: a means of quantifying the ideological "distance" between the parties over time, on a scale that ranges from −1 (the liberal pole) to 1 (the conservative pole). Scores close to 0 represent centrist ideologies.

DW-NOMINATE confirms the decades-long trend toward polarization in the House of Representatives. Since the early 1970s, according to DW-NOMINATE scores, the average ideological positions of Democrats and Republicans in the House have steadily diverged. The Democratic caucus has become more liberal. The Republican conference has become more conservative, with the pace of the GOP's rightward move accelerating after 2005.

With Democrats and Republicans more ideologically separated than ever before, compromises have become scarcer and more difficult to achieve, contributing to the current Congress' inability to get much of consequence done. In fact, the creators of the DW-Nominate methodology, Keith Poole and Howard Rosenthal, say that an examination of the trends since the origins of the U.S. Congress indicates that the House of Representatives in 2014 is more polarized than at any time since the Reconstruction era in the 1870s.

To look at data related to the modern House of Representatives, it is instructive to look at DW-NOMINATE scores from the early 1970s. In 1973–74, there was substantial overlap of ideological positions by both Republicans and Democrats. In the House of Representatives, 240 members scored in between the most conservative Democrat

Polarization in the House

These charts show the ideological scores of members of the House of Representatives, based on roll-call votes and using the DW-NOMINATE methodology. Negative numbers represent liberal views; positive numbers, conservative views.

House of Representatives, 93rd Congress (1973-74)

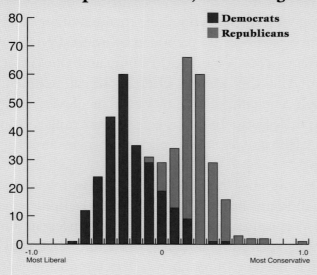

House of Representatives, 112th Congress (2011-12)

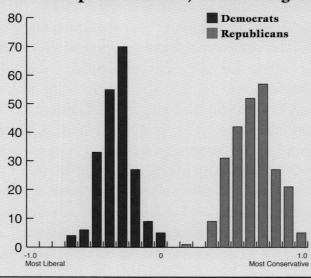

Sources: Voteview.com; Pew Research Center.

(John Rarick of Louisiana) and the most liberal Republican (Charles Whalen of Ohio).

Most experts agree that the presence of Democrats who were more conservative than their party as a whole, and of Republicans who were more liberal than theirs, helped the House function efficiently. These representatives, who fell in the center between the two parties, often proved key to consensus building and compromise.

However, by 1983–84, only 64 representatives fell between the House's most liberal Republican (Silvio Conte of Massachusetts) and its second most conservative Democrat (Charles Stenholm of Texas. Interestingly, Rep. Larry McDonald, a Democrat from Georgia, was rated more conservative than every Republican in the 98th Congress.) By 1993–94, the overlap between the most conservative Democrat and the most liberal Republican had fallen to nine House members. By 2011–12 there was no overlap at all in the House. A similar trend occurred in the U.S. Senate during the same time period.

Driving this trend toward polarization were the disappearances of moderate-to-liberal Republicans, who mainly represented the Northeast states, and conservative Democrats, who were primarily from the South. The combined House delegation of the six New England states, for instance, went from 15 Democrats and 10 Republicans in 1973–74 to 20 Democrats and two Republicans in 2011–12. In the South, the combined House delegation essentially switched positions: from 91 Democrats and 42 Republicans in 1973–74 to 107 Republicans and 47 Democrats in 2011–12.

There is no way to know whether polarization in Congress reflects a shift in ideology among the general public, or whether Congressional polarization caused the public to become more combative over ideology. Unfortunately, this distinction hardly matters. The evidence suggests that the more polarized Congress becomes, the less it is able to accomplish legislatively. In 1973–74, the 93rd Congress enacted 772 pieces of legislation. That figure has dropped in nearly every Congressional session since then, falling to 677 laws enacted by the 98th Congress (1983–84), 473 enacted by the 103rd Congress (1993–94) and just 284 enacted by the 112th Congress (2011–12).

Newly elected Speaker Paul D. Ryan shakes hands with outgoing Speaker John Boehner, October 29, 2015. Ryan, a Republican who represents Wisconsin, was the party's vice presidential candidate in 2012. He is the youngest person to hold the office of Speaker since James G. Blaine (R-Maine) in 1875.

CRISIS ENDED ... OR DEFERRED?

After McCarthy withdrew his name for the Speaker position, several other Republicans were asked to consider taking the position. All turned it down believing that the job would be nearly impossible. Finally, Wisconsin Congressman Paul Ryan reluctantly agreed to take the leadership position. However, he set several conditions. He wanted the support of the Freedom Caucus, and wanted a promise that Republicans in Congress would unite behind his leadership.

While the Freedom Caucus did not agree to endorse Ryan, after a meeting enough of the group's members felt comfortable voting for him to be the new House leader. Ryan was elected Speaker on October 29, 2015. A few days later, Congress passed a bipartisan agreement that suspended the debt ceiling until 2017. The crisis appeared to be over—at least for now.

Chapter 2

How the House Works

T he Congress of the United States is a bicameral legislature. It is made up of two bodies: the House of Representatives and the Senate. The composition and powers of the House of Representatives are established in Article 1 of the U.S. Constitution.

The House and Senate are together responsible for drafting and approving legislation that affects the entire country. Both houses of Congress must pass the bills, and the U.S. President must sign them before they take effect.

While making laws is the most important function of the House of Representatives, that body also has some powers that no other federal government entity has. Any government action that involves collecting taxes, known as "revenue bills," originate in the House of Representatives. This includes the national budget, which sets the government spending for each year. The House is also responsible for impeaching government officials, or formally accusing them of crimes committed while in office. Impeached officials must then face a trial in the U.S. Senate. Finally, the House is responsible for electing the president of the United States if there is a tie in the electoral college. This has happened twice in American history: in 1800 and in 1824.

Each U.S. state is represented in the House in proportion to its population, although every state is entitled to at least one representative. The states elect a total of 435 representatives. The most populous state, California, has 53 representatives in the 114th Congress (2015–2017). Seven states—Alaska, Delaware, Montana, North Dakota, South Dakota, Vermont, and Wyoming—have only one representative in the House.

In addition to the state representatives, there are six non-voting members of the House. Five are elected from U.S. overseas territories—Puerto Rico, American Samoa, the Virgin Islands, Guam, and the Northern Mariana Islands. The sixth is elected to represent the District of Columbia. These representatives are generally allowed to work and vote in House committees, but may not vote with the full House to pass legislation.

The requirements to serve in the House of Representatives are lower than the requirements for election to the Senate or for president or vice president. Representatives must be 25 years or older and have been a U.S. citizen for at least seven years.

The youngest member of the 114th Congress (2015–2017) is Elise Stefanik, a Republican who represent's New York's 21st Congressional District. She was 30 years old when she was originally elected in 2014.

Representatives serve two-year terms, and all seats in the House are up for election at the same time. This time frame was set in the Constitution. The authors believed that the House needed to have more frequent elections so that it could best represent the immediate needs of citizens. U.S. Senators, by comparison, are elected to six-year terms. The Senate is expected to be a more deliberative branch of the legislature.

A political party that holds at least 218 seats in the House of Representatives is called the majority party. The party with less than half of the seats is known as the minority party. The majority party has a lot of power, and essentially controls the way the House operates.

Representative Keith Ellison (D-Minn.) greets constituents at a parade in Golden Valley, Minnesota. Because members of the House of Representatives are elected every two years, they must campaign frequently and stay in touch with the needs of people living in their district if they wish to retain their seats in Congress.

THE HOUSE LEADERSHIP STRUCTURE

The Speaker of the House is elected by all members of the House. Typically, the Speaker is a leading member of the majority party, and generally serves as the party's primary spokesperson in Congress. The Speaker has enormous power because he or she sets the agenda for the House by deciding what legislation that assembly will consider. The Speaker also presides over all debate in the House, decides whether procedures are being properly followed, and can appoint special committees and task forces to deal with unexpected issues that arise.

Members of the majority and minority parties meet separately to select their leaders and discuss matters that are important to the party. Democrats call their meeting a caucus; Republicans prefer the term convention. Each party has a leader (known as the Majority Leader or Minority Leader, depending on which party holds the most seats in the House) who represents the party on the House floor. The Minority Leader also serves as the party's primary spokesman in Congress.

The Majority and Minority Leaders of each party are assisted by officers called Whips. The name *whip* comes from a old hunting term, "whipping in," which referred to a person who would use a whip to keep a pack of hunting dogs together following the scent of prey. The Majority Whip and the Minority Whip are responsible for making sure all members of their party vote according to the party's official policy. They can encourage representatives by offering them special

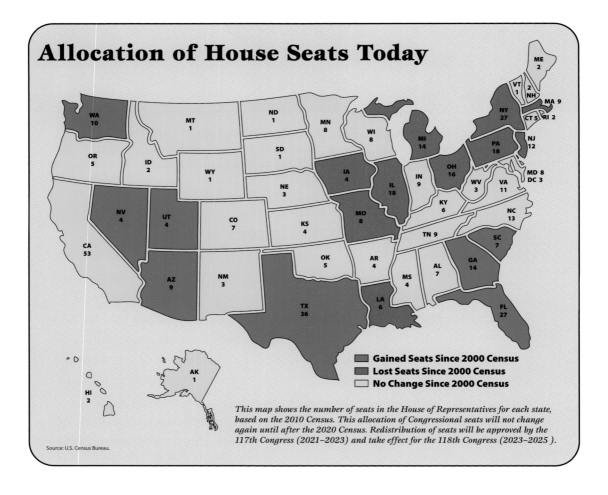

Allocation of House Seats Today

ME 2
VT 1
NH 2
WA 10
MT 1
ND 1
MN 8
WI 8
NY 27
MA 9
CT 5
RI 2
NJ 12
MI 14
PA 18
OR 5
ID 2
SD 1
OH 16
MD 8
DC 3
WY 1
IA 4
IN 9
WV 3
VA 11
NE 3
IL 18
KY 6
NV 4
UT 4
CO 7
MO 8
NC 13
CA 53
KS 4
TN 9
SC 7
AZ 9
NM 3
OK 5
AR 4
AL 7
GA 14
MS 4
LA 6
FL 27
TX 36
AK 1
HI 2

- Gained Seats Since 2000 Census
- Lost Seats Since 2000 Census
- No Change Since 2000 Census

This map shows the number of seats in the House of Representatives for each state, based on the 2010 Census. This allocation of Congressional seats will not change again until after the 2020 Census. Redistribution of seats will be approved by the 117th Congress (2021–2023) and take effect for the 118th Congress (2023–2025).

Source: U.S. Census Bureau.

In the 114th Congress, Republican Steve Scalise of Louisiana (left) holds the position of Majority Whip, while Democrat Steny Hoyer of Maryland (right) serves as the Minority Whip.

favors or privileges, such as assignments to important House committees, so long as they vote with the rest of the party. They can also threaten to take away committee assignments and other privileges if a representative votes against what the party wants.

The Speaker, party leaders, and whips are given special offices in the U.S. Capitol building. They also tend to move up when there are changes at the top of the leadership structure. For example, if the minority party gains control of Congress by winning more than 218 seats in an election, the Minority Leader will often become the next Speaker of the House. The Minority Whip may move up into the vacated position of Majority Leader.

Other important positions in the House include the Republican Conference Chairman and the Democratic Caucus Chairman, who manage their party's meetings at which leaders are elected. The chairmen also handle the distribution of committee assignments and help to set the party's legislative priorities. The Republican Conference Chairman is considered that party's third most important member of the House leadership structure. On the Democratic side, the third most important position is Assistant Democratic Leader, which was created in 2011 to help the party leader.

Although the American political system is dominated by the Republican and Democratic parties, there have been a handful of representatives who were independent of the two parties. Bernie Sanders of Vermont was elected to the House as an independent candidate in

Nancy Pelosi, a Democrat from California, is the only woman to serve as Speaker of the House. She held the position from 2007 to 2011, when Republicans gained control of the chamber. Since then, Pelosi has been the Minority Leader.

1990, and served in the House until 2007. More commonly, a member of one of the parties may decide to renounce his or her affiliation and become an independent. In 2000, for example, Representative Virgil Goode, who had previously been elected as a Democrat, left the party and was re-elected as an independent candidate. Independents generally join either the Republican conference (as Goode did) or the Democratic caucus (as Sanders did), and agree to vote with members of the larger on important matters in order to receive committee assignments.

WORKING THROUGH COMMITTEES

The House conducts most of its work through a system of small groups, called committees. Today there are 20 standing committees of the House. Eighteen of them deal with areas of policy, including Agriculture; Appropriations; Armed Services; the Budget; Education and the Workforce; Energy and Commerce; Financial Services; Foreign Affairs; Homeland Security; House Administration; the Judiciary; Natural Resources; Oversight and Government Reform; Science, Space, and Technology; Small Business; Transportation and Infrastructure; Veterans' Affairs; and Ways and Means. The committees meet to discuss proposed legislation, They also oversee government agencies, programs, and activities related to the committee's policy jurisdiction.

The Rules Committee is a standing committee that does not have a specific policy area. Instead, the Rules Committee determines when a bill, or proposed law, will be discussed by the full House of Representatives. The Rules Committee also sets the conditions for each bill, determining how much time will be allowed for discussion and whether changes, or amendments, to the bill will be permitted. This control over the process of making laws means that the Rules Committee is very powerful, so it is usually dominated by members of the majority party. The Speaker may decide to stock the Rules Committee with representatives that he trusts to carry out his agenda for the House.

The House Ethics Committee, on the other hand, is made up of equal numbers of Republicans and Democrats. This committee sets restrictions on the behavior of House members so that they are aware of conflicts of interest related to gifts, travel, or campaign activities. The committee investigates whether members have violated the ethics standards, and recommends to the entire House what action should be taken. The committee may determine that the member did nothing wrong, or they can vote to issue a formal statement of disapproval, called censure, to a House member who has broken the rules. This occurred most recently in 2010, when Representative Charlie Rangel (D-NY) was censured for 11 violations of ethics rules related to his failure to comply with federal tax laws.

The Speaker of the House is one of the most powerful elected officials in the federal government. According to the U.S. Constitution, if both the president and vice president become incapable of continuing in office due to death, impeachment, or other reasons, the Speaker of the House would become president of the United States. However, this situation has never happened in American history. James K. Polk, a Democrat who served as Speaker of the House from 1835 to 1839, is the only former Speaker to serve as president, being elected in 1844.

In the worst cases, the Ethics Committee can recommend that a member be expelled from the House. This has only happened five times in American history. Three occurred in 1861, when representatives from Missouri and Kentucky were expelled for their support of the Confederate States of America during the Civil War. In 1980 Representative Michael J. Myers (D-PA) was expelled from the house after being caught by the FBI accepting a $50,000 bribe in what became known as the ABSCAM scandal. After leaving Congress, Myers was sentenced to three years in prison. In 2002, Representative James Traficant (D-Ohio) was convicted in a federal court of bribery, racketeering, and tax evasion, and was expelled from the House.

Nearly all of the standing committees are broken into multiple subcommittees that deal with one aspect of the committee's work. For example, the House Education and the Workforce Committee includes four subcommittees, which deal with Early Childhood, Elementary and Secondary Education; Health, Employment, Labor, and Pensions; Higher Education and Workforce Training; and Workforce Protections. The House Foreign Affairs Committee has subcommittees that deal with world regions as well as specific threats. The subcommittees include Africa, Global Health, Global Human Rights and International Organizations; Asia and the Pacific; Europe, Eurasia and Emerging Threats; Middle East and North Africa; Terrorism, Nonproliferation, and Trade; and Western Hemisphere.

Party leaders in the House of Representatives assign members to committees. The total number of committee slots allotted to each party is about the same as the ratio of seats between the two parties in the House. For example, in the 114th Congress (2015–2017), the Republicans held 247 seats, or almost 57 percent of the total membership of the House, so the Republicans will tend to have about 57 percent of the seats on every committee. This is an average—some important or prestigious committees will have greater numbers of majority party representatives. For example, the Ways and Means Committee, which writes all legislation involving tax revenue, has 24 Republican members and 15 Democrats in the 114th Congress. Thus Republicans make up 62 percent of that committee's total membership. The majority party does this to ensure that it can always control that committee's activities.

Each committee is led by a chairperson, who is chosen by the party leadership and is a member of the majority party. The chairs are often awarded on the basis of seniority, with those who have been serving in the House the longest receiving priority. The Republican Party is more likely than the Democratic Party to elevate representatives to committee chair positions without regard to seniority. They do this to reward those who raise large amounts of money for the party, or who regularly vote the way that the leadership wants.

SPECIAL COMMITTEES

When necessary, leaders of the House of Representatives can establish a committee to deal with a problem or special issue. These are known as select committees. Select committees are usually formed to conduct investigations or to study an issue that one of the standing committees cannot address comprehensively. For example, in 2014 the House Select Committee on Benghazi was created to investigate all the circumstances surrounding a September 2012 terrorist attack on the U.S. Embassy in Benghazi, Libya. Several Americans were killed in that attack, including U.S. Ambassador J. Christopher Stevens. This committee gathers testimony from people who were at the embassy, as well as high-ranking government officials, to determine what went wrong at Benghazi. It is intended to be a temporary committee that will cease to exist when its work is complete.

On the other hand, the work of the House Permanent Select Committee on Intelligence never ends. This committee is responsible for reviewing and approving the undercover activities of U.S. intelligence agencies, such as the Central

Republican Trey Gowdy of South Carolina is chairman of the House Select Committee on Benghazi.

Intelligence Agency (CIA), the National Security Agency (NSA), and similar agencies within the Department of Homeland Security and the Department of Defense. It was established in the late 1970s due to the discovery of illegal activities being conducted by members of those secretive agencies.

House members are also involved in several "joint committees" that also include members of the Senate. Members of the Joint Economic Committee review economic conditions and recommend improvements in economic policy. The Joint Committee on Taxation works with experts to make sure any legislation that includes revenue or tax components are fully vetted and understood. The Joint Committee on the Library oversees the operations of the Library of Congress, as well as the federal government's art collection and botanical gardens. and the Joint Committee on Printing oversees the operations of the U.S. Government Publishing Office (GPO), which prints copies of every bill for Congressional review and is the main printing organization for all federal agencies.

CREATING LEGISLATION

The most important duty of the House of Representatives is to write the laws under which the United States functions. All federal laws begin with a bill, or draft of the proposed legislation. The idea for a bill can come from a member of Congress, from the president, from an advocacy group, or from a private citizen who suggests the idea. The congressperson and his staff research the idea and write the bill. Then the bill's author meets with other members of Congress and asks them to support the bill.

To be considered by the House of Representatives, a bill must be sponsored by a member of the House. The sponsor introduces a bill by placing it into a box, known as a "hopper," at the desk of the Clerk, the chief record-keeper of the House. Each bill is numbered in the order it was received and read during the two-year Congressional session. For example, H.R.10 would be the tenth bill read in the House of Representatives during that session of Congress. Thousands of bills are introduced in the House of Representatives each year.

A joint session of Congress in the House chamber at the U.S. Capitol.

Once a bill has been numbered and read, the Speaker of the House assigns the bill to one of the House's standing committees. A bill can be referred to more than one committee, and it can be split so that parts are sent to different committees.

Members of the committee review, research, and revise each bill that they receive. Often, bills are assigned to a subcommittee, where they can be examined more carefully. Subcommittees will seek expert opinions as they consider the bill, and may hold hearings in which experts testify about the pros and cons of the legislation. When the subcommittee finishes its work, the bill may be sent back to the full committee for consideration. If most of the committee's members believe that the bill is ready to become a law, they will vote to send it back to the larger House for discussion. However, a committee may decide that a bill is not ready to become a law, and can keep it under discussion in the committee until the end of the two-year Congressional session. Such bills are said to have "died in committee," and must be reintroduced during the next session of Congress to be considered again. Most bills that are introduced never make it out of the committee stage.

When a committee sends a bill to the House floor, it also prepares a report explaining why the committee supports the bill. Committee members who oppose a bill sometimes write a dissenting opinion in the report. This report is sent to the whole chamber, and time is scheduled for the House to discuss the bill and vote on it.

The representatives have a chance to read the bill before they vote. They also have a chance to tell others why they support or oppose it. The representatives can also recommend changes. When all the changes that have been made, the bill is ready for a vote.

Representatives can vote "yes" or "no" on a bill. They also have the option of voting "present" if they want to indicate that they are in the chamber but don't want to take a position on the bill, perhaps because of a conflict of interest. A majority of the House members, or 218 members, must be present in the chamber in order for a bill to be voted on. This is called a quorum. If a majority of the quorum votes "yes," the bill passes in the House of Representatives. It is then certified by the House clerk and sent to the U.S. Senate.

Bills have to be approved by both the House and the Senate in order to become laws. A bill that has been passed by both houses is sent to the president. He then has several choices. The president can sign the bill, and it becomes a law. Or the president can veto, or refuse to sign, the bill. When this happens, the bill does not become a law. However, it is sent back to Congress, and another vote can be held on the bill. If two-thirds of the representatives and senators vote to support the bill, they override the president's veto and the bill becomes a law.

IMPEACHMENT

One power that is exclusive to the House of Representatives is impeachment—making formal charges against a high-ranking government official for crimes committed while he or she is in office. Officials subject to impeachment can be either elected (such as the president or vice president) or appointed (such as federal judges and the heads of government departments).

If a member of the House believes that an official is doing wrong, he or she can start an impeachment investigation by introducing a bill in Congress. Or, the House may receive a request for impeachment from other members of the federal government that requires an investigation, and pass a resolution authorizing an inquiry.

The House Judiciary Committee has jurisdiction over impeachments. After a thorough investigation, members of the committee must decide whether to pursue articles of impeachment against the accused official and report them to the full House. If the committee believes the matter is serious, it presents the articles of impeachment to the House for a vote. If a majority of the House votes to adopt the articles of impeachment, the House will appoint members—usually also from the Judiciary Committee—to manage the impeachment trial in the Senate. These managers act as prosecutors who will present the House's evidence that the accused official is guilty of the charges.

An official that is impeached by the House faces a trial in the U.S. Senate. If found guilty of the charges, that official is removed from office and may be disqualified from holding office in the future.

President Richard M. Nixon announces that he will release tapes of his private White House conversations during the Watergate investigation, April 1974. As the House prepared to vote on impeachment, Nixon decided to resign the presidency in August of that year.

However, there are no fines or prison sentences for those who are found guilty of impeachable offenses. Those must be determined by a separate trial in a civil or criminal court.

Impeachment is a fairly rare occurrence in American history. The House has voted on articles of impeachment more than 60 times, but only 19 have resulted in impeachments. Fifteen of those cases involved federal judges; eight of those judges were subsequently found guilty in the Senate and removed from office. The most recent was Thomas Porteous, a federal judge from Louisiana, who was impeached and removed from the bench in 2010.

Only four other government officials have been impeached by the House—U.S. Senator William Blount of North Carolina in 1797, U.S. Secretary of War William Belknap in 1876, President Andrew Johnson in 1868, and President Bill Clinton in 1998. None were found guilty, although the Senate expelled Blount anyway.

The most famous cases of impeachment are those involving the presidents. Both Johnson and Clinton were acquitted after trials in the Senate. Richard Nixon resigned from office before the House completed its impeachment process. Impeachment bills have been filed against other presidents. In 2012 and 2013, for example, some Republicans formally requested impeachment of President Obama, but the Judiciary Committee's investigation found that he had not committed any crimes worthy of reporting to the full House.

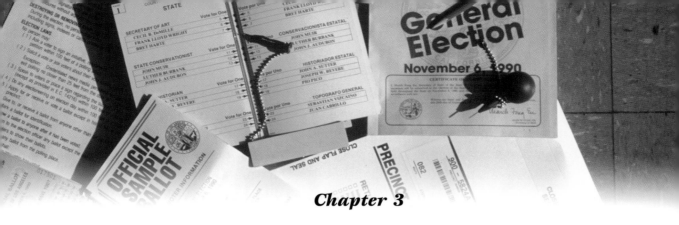

Chapter 3

Conflict and Compromise

During the Great Depression of the 1930s, Democrats gained firm control over the House of Representatives. Many Democrats were elected to the House because of broad public support for the New Deal policies of Franklin D. Roosevelt, who was president from 1933 to 1945. But for approximately five decades after Roosevelt's death, the Democratic Party maintained its hold on the House. In fact, between 1933 and 1994, Republicans held a majority in the House only two times: in the 80th congress (1947–49) and the 83rd Congress (1953–55), at the start of President Dwight D. Eisenhower's first term in the White House.

Although Republicans were the minority party, they often had enough strength in the House to block any legislation that was considered too liberal. Democrats, meanwhile, worked with the Republicans to pass bills for the good of the country. In fact, about 80 percent of the proposals that Eisenhower, a Republican, sent to Congress were ultimately enacted into law. These included the Federal Aid Highway Act of 1956, which created the modern system of interstate highways, and the Civil Rights Act of 1957, the first legislation related to protecting African American voting rights since the 1870s.

CIVIL RIGHTS BATTLES

Civil rights legislation became a contentious matter during the 1950s and 1960s. Often, Southern Democrats in the House would try to block or weaken any legislation that would have given greater rights to African Americans, or would have imposed integration of schools and public places. In 1956, in response to the Supreme Court's ruling in *Brown v. Board of Education of Topeka* (1954) that segregation of schools was unconstitutional, 82 of the 110 representatives from the Southern states signed a statement called the Southern Manifesto that opposed the Court's decision. Nineteen senators also signed the document, in which they promised to use all legal means to prevent racial integration.

A key member of this effort was Howard Smith, a Democrat from Virginia who had signed the Southern Manifesto. As chairman of the powerful Rules Committee from 1955 to 1967, Smith controlled the flow of legislation to the House. He used his position to stall civil rights bills in his committee in order to prevent them from reaching the House floor for a vote. More than a hundred civil rights bills died in committee, while others had important elements stripped from them so that they became ineffective.

During the 1950s, another Southern Democrat named Sam Rayburn was one of the most powerful men in Congress. Rayburn served as Speaker of the House whenever Democrats controlled the chamber between 1940 and his death in 1961—a total of 17 years. Rayburn was known for his honesty and integrity, and after the *Brown v. Board of Education* decision he had come to believe that continuing

When Alaska and Hawaii were admitted as states in 1959, the membership of the House temporarily increased to 437. One representative was seated from both states in the 87th Congress (1961–63), but apportionment of the other 435 seats remained unchanged. The makeup of the House would remain at 437 until reapportionment resulting from the 1960 census took effect in the 88th Congress (1963–65).

the policies of segregation and repression of the Black vote were unfair. In the late 1950s he began to support civil rights legislation, and he also tried to change the House rules to make it more difficult to stop the legislation from proceeding. For example, at one point Rayburn implemented the "Twenty-one Day Rule," which gave the Rules Committee three weeks to bring bills to the House floor for a vote. This measure, and others, were meant to speed up the movement of legislation. However, the Twenty-one Day Rule proved to be ineffective and was soon repealed.

Sam Rayburn's 17 years as Speaker of the House are the most in Congress's history, and he is the only person to ever serve more than two non-consecutive terms in the position. Rayburn was widely respected by his peers in the House. A building built in 1965 that houses the Congressional offices of 169 representatives is named in his memory.

With Rayburn's backing, the Civil Rights Act of 1957 passed the House by a vote of 285 to 126. It established the U.S. Commission on Civil Rights, which was scheduled to meet for two years. The act also created a civil rights division in the U.S. Justice Department, and authorized the U.S. Attorney General to seek federal court injunctions to protect the voting rights of African Americans.

However, although the Southern Democrats had not been able to stop the bill, they did manage to remove certain provisions that made it difficult to enforce the new law. To remedy this, Congress passed another law, the Civil Rights Act of 1960. Again, however, this legislation was weakened as it passed through Congress.

By 1963, the civil rights movement had gained momentum. President John F. Kennedy gave a speech encouraging Congress to pass a more comprehensive civil rights bill. On June 20, 1963, Emanuel Celler (D–NY) introduced a new civil rights bill in the

House. It was initially reviewed by the Judicial Committee. In November 1963, following House procedure, it was sent to the Rules Committee, chaired by Howard Smith.

It seemed likely that this bill would suffer the same fate as previous civil rights legislation. However, on November 22, 1963, Kennedy was assassinated in Dallas. The nation mourned the slain president. Kennedy's vice president, Lyndon B. Johnson, had previously been a supporter of civil rights in the Senate. Four days after being sworn in as president, Johnson spoke to the members of Congress. "No memorial oration or eulogy could more eloquently honor President Kennedy's memory than the earliest possible passage of the civil rights bill for which he fought so long," he said. Johnson spoke privately with members of the House and Senate, asking them to let the bill move forward. Both houses of Congress passed the bill, and on July 2, 1964, Johnson signed the Civil Rights Act of 1964.

The Civil Rights Act of 1964 outlawed discrimination based on an individual's race, color, religion, sex, or national origin. The Act outlawed segregation in businesses such as theaters, restaurants, and hotels. It banned discriminatory practices in hiring, promoting, setting wages, and firing employees. And it outlawed segregation in public facilities such as swimming pools, libraries, and public schools.

African Americans weren't the only ones who would benefit from the Civil Rights Act. Women, religious minorities, and Hispanics also benefited from this landmark legislation. The Civil Rights Act would later serve as a model for other anti-discrimination measures passed by Congress, including the Pregnancy Discrimination Act of 1978 and the Americans with Disabilities Act of 1990.

Congress followed this law the next year with the Voting Rights Act of 1965. It called for federal workers to register black voters, and it prohibited the use of literacy tests as a condition for voting. Thanks to the protection offered by this legislation, the number of African-Americans registered to vote soared throughout the nation. By the end of 1965, 250,000 new black voters had been registered. Other federal legislation would ensure that congressional districts would be drawn in a way that properly represented African Americans. These impor-

Representative Shirley Chisholm (right) attends an event with civil rights pioneer Rosa Parks during the 1970s. Chisholm was the first African-American woman elected to the House of Representatives. She repre- sented a New York district in the House from 1969 to 1983.

tant laws ensured that African Americans would have a more appro- priate role in their government.

PROTECTING THE PUBLIC INTEREST

The American public was galvanized in the early 1970s when news broke about a scandal involving the president of the United States, Republican Richard M. Nixon. On June 17, 1972, five men were caught breaking into the Watergate building in Washington, D.C., where the Democratic Party had its offices. Investigators later learned that the men had been working for advisers to President Nixon's re-election campaign. They were looking for information that would make the Democratic candidates look bad.

As news reporters dug further into the Watergate break-in, they uncovered more illegal acts. The president himself was involved. Although he did not order the Watergate break-in, Nixon tried to cover up the fact that his aides had hired the burglars. In February 1974, the House Judiciary Committee began to investigate the matter and held public hearings on the scandal.

In July 1974, the Judiciary Committee approved the first of three articles of impeachment against Nixon. The president was accused of obstructing justice, abusing presidential power, and contempt of

Congress. Before the full House could vote on the articles, however, Nixon resigned from office on August 9, 1974.

The Watergate scandal shook the American public's faith in its government. Yet Watergate also showed that the Constitution worked as it had been intended, and that no one—not even the president of the United States—was above the law.

The House would continue to exercise its investigative and oversight responsibilities throughout the 1970s. In 1975, the House Select Committee on Intelligence was formed to investigate alleged illegal activities committed by the Central Intelligence Agency (CIA), Federal Bureau of Investigation (FBI), and the National Security Agency (NSA). From 1976 to 1977 this committee was known as the Pike Commission, after its chairman, Democrat Otis G. Pike of New York. The Pike Commission was officially dissolved when the 94th Congress ended in January 1977, so the House subsequently decided to make the select committee permanent. The 95th Congress followed up on the work of the Pike Commission by passing the Foreign Intelligence Surveillance Act of 1978. This legislation required government agencies to follow specific procedures when gathering intelligence on foreign agents, as well as on American citizens or foreigners living in the United States.

In the 95th Congress (1977–1979), the House Select Committee on Assassinations was formed to investigate the killing of President Kennedy in 1963 and of Martin Luther King Jr. in 1968. The Committee released a report in 1978 which indicated that Kennedy had been killed as part of a conspiracy, contradicting the official verdict issued by the Warren Commission during the 1960s.

PARTISAN POLITICS

Jimmy Carter's victory in the 1976 presidential election gave the Democratic Party control of the White House as well as both houses of Congress. The Democrats held more than 60 percent of the seats in both the House and Senate, which meant that the party had an excellent opportunity to pass major legislation related to health care and employment. But although Congress did pass some important energy bills, the Democrats were never able to deliver on their health-care proposals. In part this was due to Carter's differences with House Speaker Thomas "Tip" O'Neill of Massachusetts. The president wanted to reduce government spending, while the speaker wanted to increase it.

Ideologically, O'Neill and Carter's successor as president, Ronald Reagan, could not have been more different. O'Neill was strongly critical of Reagan, once calling him the worst president that he had known in his political career. Yet the two politicians were able to find common ground and work together. In 1981, Congress approved a budget with bipartisan support that included the greatest increase in defense spending in American history, together with huge cutbacks in domestic programs. On the other hand, the following year Congress passed the Tax Equity and Fiscal Responsibility Act of 1982, which has been described as the "largest tax increase in history."

President Gerald Ford delivers the annual State of the Union Address to Congress, 1975. Seated behind him are vice president Nelson Rockefeller and Speaker of the House Carl Albert (D-Okla.). Ford took an unprecedented path from the House of Representatives to the White House. The longtime Republican congressman from Michigan was serving as House Minority Leader in 1973 when Nixon's vice president, Spiro Agnew, resigned from office due to charges of bribery and tax fraud. Nixon appointed Ford to fill the vacant vice president's position, and he was confirmed by Congress. When Nixon himself resigned, Ford became president as specified by the Constitution. He ran for a full term in 1976, but lost in a close race to Democrat Jimmy Carter.

Tip O'Neill's most famous aphorism, "All politics is local," was a reminder to politicians that they needed to listen to their constituents and address the issues that were important to them. O'Neill served as Speaker from 1977 to his retirement in 1987, the second-longest tenure in the history of the House.

Perhaps the best example of how Reagan and O'Neill were able to work together came in 1983. Reagan, as a conservative, was strongly opposed to Social Security, viewing it as an expensive example of "big government." O'Neill and other liberals cherished Social Security as one of the great accomplishments of Roosevelt's New Deal. The Social Security program was popular among most Americans, and was supported by large majorities in both houses of Congress. Early in his first term, Reagan's economic advisers determined that at the current rate of spending, the Social Security trust fund could run out of money by 1983. Reagan could have let the program collapse; instead, he worked with O'Neill to establish a bipartisan commission in 1981 to determine ways to keep Social Security operating for the long term.

The National Commission on Social Security Reform, chaired by Alan Greenspan, issued its report in January 1983. The Commission's recommendations became the basis for legislation that originated in the House to fix the Social Security system and resolved the financing problem. Changes included raising the retirement age from 65 to 67, and requiring government employees to pay into Social Security for the first time. "This bill demonstrates for all time our nation's ironclad commitment to Social Security," Reagan announced when he signed the bill.

During the 1980s and early 1990s, the Democratic Party maintained control of the House, while control of the Senate swung from the Republicans to the Democrats and back again. But all that would change in the 1994 midterm election.

Chapter 4

A House Divided, 1993-Present

In January 1993, Democrat Bill Clinton was sworn in as president of the United States. In the 103rd Congress which convened that same month, the Democratic Party held large majorities in both House (270 to 164) and Senate (57 to 43). With control of two branches of government, this appeared to be the best opportunity for the Democratic Party to achieve its legislative goals, including health care reform, since the Carter administration of the late 1970s.

However, the opportunities did not materialize in the way that Democrats had hoped. Clinton pushed for a budget in 1993 that included a major tax increase and was very unpopular. The budget passed by just a single vote in each house of Congress. The president also blundered by appointing his wife, Hillary Rodham Clinton, to head a Task Force on National Health Care Reform in September 1993. The group drafted a bill for Congress that was more than 1,000 pages long, and would have established an enormous government bureaucracy to oversee health care. Republicans and even many Democrats opposed the plan, offering their own alternatives. By mid-1994 it was clear that the health care reform bill could not pass through Congress.

Clinton had been elected president in 1992 with less than 50 percent of the vote, and his popularity fell even further due to mistakes and scandals. A Gallup survey conducted during the first week of September 1994 showed just 39 percent of Americans approved of the way Clinton was handling his job, while 54 percent disapproved. The Democratic-led Congress was viewed even less favorably, with just 21 percent of Americans approving of the way it was doing its job according to a Gallup Poll from October 1994. The House's reputation was tarnished by a number of scandals involving representatives, including a mail fraud that involved the chairman of the powerful Ways and Means Committee, Dan Rostenkowski (D-Ill.). Americans were unhappy with the direction of government and ready for change.

THE REPUBLICAN REVOLUTION

Republican congressman Newt Gingrich of Georgia, the party's whip in the House, believed that Republicans could take advantage of public anger at the Democrats. While campaigning for the 1994 midterm elections, Gingrich and other Republicans unveiled the Contract with America. It outlined 10 bills the Republicans promised to introduce in the first 100 days of the new Congress if they won a majority. These included measures that would check spending by requiring a balanced budget, reform the welfare system, and establish term limits for members of Congress.

On Election Day, the Republicans won an astonishing victory. They gained 54 seats in the House, gaining control of the chamber for the first time since 1955. The Republicans also gained control of the Senate. The press called this event the "Republican Revolution." When the 104th Congress opened, Gingrich was elected Speaker.

Gingrich and the Republicans soon brought the Contract with America bills to the floor of the House. Nine of the bills passed the House, but most of the legislation languished in the Senate.

The Republican Revolution placed President Clinton in an awkward position. Without Democratic control of Congress, he would be even less likely to accomplish his legislative goals. Over the next four years, the White House would engage in a series of political battles

House Speaker Newt Gingrich (right) and Vice President Al Gore look on as President Bill Clinton delivers the 1995 State of the Union Address. Gingrich was the leader of the 1994 Republican Revolution that gave his party control of the House for the first time in four decades.

with Gingrich and the House Republicans. In late 1995 and early 1996, disagreements over the budget resulted in a pair of government shutdowns.

Yet the two parties were also able to work together to accomplish meaningful legislation at times. In 1996, Congress passed the Personal Responsibility and Work Opportunity Act. This legislation reformed the welfare system, setting a five-year limit on welfare benefits and requiring able-bodied recipients to find employment. Its passage fulfilled a promise that Clinton had made while campaigning for president in 1992 to "end welfare as we know it," while also fulfilling one of the key promises of the Republican Contract with America.

Clinton won a second term as president in 1996, but Republicans maintained their majority in the House. Over the next four years, the two parties were able to make some significant compromises on legislation. For example, the Balanced Budget Act of 1997 included reductions in spending on Medicare and Medicaid, which the GOP favored. But the act also established a new federal program that Clinton advocated—health insurance for children whose families earned too much to qualify for Medicaid but too little to afford private insurance.

SCANDALS, CENSURE, AND IMPEACHMENT

Scandal was in the headlines throughout much of Clinton's second term as president. In 1994, an independent counsel had been appointed to investigate Clinton's involvement in a failed real-estate development deal known as Whitewater. The independent council, Kenneth Starr, soon broadened the scope of the investigation into other areas of Clinton's life. In September 1998, Starr issued a report that outlined 11 possible grounds on which Clinton could be impeached. These included obstruction of justice and lying under oath (perjury) related to a sexual affair the president had conducted with a White House intern. A few weeks later, the House Judiciary Committee voted to investigate whether the president should be impeached.

The investigation did not help the Republicans in the November 1998 midterm elections, however. The party had been expecting to gain seats in the House. Instead, the Democrats picked up five seats, although the Republicans maintained their majority for the third consecutive election.

Gingrich took the blame for the poor showing, and a few days later resigned his post as Speaker. Like Clinton, Gingrich was dogged by his own scandals, and in 1997 the Speaker was censured by the House for ethical violations. Although he won re-election in 1998, Gingrich decided to resign from Congress altogether in early 1999.

Bob Livingston of Louisiana was chosen by the Republicans to succeed Gingrich as Speaker when the next Congress convened. Livingston had been one of the leading supporters of impeaching Clinton. However, when news that Livingston had conducted his own extramarital affair became public, he declined the Speaker position and resigned from the House.

Despite the turmoil, the House approved two articles of impeachment against Clinton on December 19, 1998. The chairman of the Judiciary Committee, Henry Hyde (R-Ill.), led a team of representatives who presented the case before the Senate during January and

February of 1999. Ultimately, the Senate acquitted Clinton of both charges on February 12, 1999.

THE BUSH ERA BEGINS

The 2000 presidential election was one of the closest in U.S. history. Vice President Al Gore, the Democratic Party candidate, won slightly more votes nationally than George W. Bush, the Republican Party candidate. However, when Bush was determined to be the winner in Florida, that state's 25 electoral votes gave him enough to win the presidency. The Republican Party also maintained its majority in the House for the fourth straight election—the longest streak since the 1920s. The gap between the Republicans (221 seats) and Democrats (212 seats) had narrowed considerably, however.

With slim majorities in both houses of Congress, President Bush succeeded in getting some important domestic legislation enacted during his first years in office. In June 2001, he signed into law the Economic Growth and Tax Relief Reconciliation Act (EGTRRA), which lowered income-tax rates and the estate tax. President Bush also pushed for the Medicare Prescription Drug, Improvement, and Modernization Act, which subsidized the cost of prescription medica-

Early in his first term, Bush worked with Republican and Democratic leaders in Congress to pass the No Child Left Behind Act of 2001. This legislation marked a significant increase in federal spending on education. The bill was sponsored by Representatives John Boehner (R-Ohio) and George Miller (D-Calif.), and Senators Ted Kennedy (D-Mass.) and Judd Gregg (R-NH).

tions for older Americans. After much debate, Congress passed this legislation in late 2003.

But the focus of Bush's presidency soon changed. On September 11, 2001, terrorists belonging to a group called al-Qaeda hijacked four passenger airplanes and crashed them into the World Trade Center in New York City and the Pentagon, outside Washington, D.C. The attacks killed nearly 3,000 people. Three days after the attacks, Congress passed a joint resolution authorizing the president "to use all necessary and appropriate force against those nations, organizations, or persons he determines planned, authorized, committed, or aided the terrorist attacks." The next month, Bush ordered an invasion of Afghanistan, because its government was sheltering the al-Qaeda leaders who had planned the September 11 attacks.

At home, the government took other steps to prevent future terrorist attacks. On October 24, 2001, the House passed the USA PATRIOT Act by a vote of 357 to 66. The next day, the legislation passed in the Senate and the following day President Bush signed it into law. The USA PATRIOT Act gave government agencies more power to collect information on American citizens. It was hoped that this would help catch terrorists before they struck. However, concerns soon arose about government surveillance of American citizens.

Bush also sought to send the U.S. military to Iraq to depose dictator Saddam Hussein, who he believed was harboring weapons of mass destruction that terrorists might use against the United States. He asked Congress for a formal resolution authorizing the U.S. to go to war against Iraq if needed. The resolution was passed by Congress in October 2002, with nearly every Republican representative and 40 percent of the Democrats voting in favor of the measure.

Many voters appreciated the Bush administration's actions, and in the 2002 midterm elections the Republican Party increased its majority in the House by gaining eight seats.

THINGS FALL APART

In March 2003, the United States invaded Iraq. In a matter of weeks, Saddam Hussein's government had fallen. However, the military victory proved to be the easy part. Over the next two years, Iraq descended into chaos, with former supporters of Saddam mounting a violent insurgency, al-Qaeda taking root in Iraq, and a savage civil war erupting between Iraq's Sunni Muslim minority and its Shia Muslim majority.

In spite of the deteriorating situation in Iraq—and the failure to find any WMD there—Republicans fared well in the 2004 elections. The GOP picked up three seats in the House and four in the Senate. Bush also won election to a second term.

However, Iraq would remain a problem for the Republican Party during Bush's second term. As American casualties increased, and it was clear there was no easy way out of the situation, Bush's favorability steadily declined, and so did that of the House Republicans.

By the time the 2006 midterm elections arrived, opinion polls showed that most Americans considered the Iraq War a mistake. And the Republican Party paid the price, losing 30 seats in the House of Representatives and six seats in the Senate. For the first time since 1994, Democrats had regained control of both chambers of Congress.

DEMOCRATS IN CONTROL

As the Democrats took control of the 110th Congress (2007–2009), the party made history by electing Nancy Pelosi, a representative from California, the first female Speaker of the House. Before the session began, Pelosi promised that the Democrats would vote on eight major bills during the first six days that Congress was in session, a period of roughly 100 working hours. The party did in fact pass the bills listed in Pelosi's "100-Hour Plan," although they still required passage by the Senate to become law. Most of this legislation did eventually pass in the Senate as well, including an increase in the minimum wage to $7.25, new rules to reduce the influence of lobbyists in Congress, and a "pay-as-you-go" requirement that future tax cuts had to be paid for with equivalent cuts to government spending, rather than new debt.

During the final years of the Bush administration, the country became mired in the worst economic depression since the 1930s. Congress and the president worked together to pass the Emergency

Economic Stabilization Act of 2008. This legislation allowed the government to borrow $700 billion and invest the money in businesses that were in financial trouble. A fund, called the Troubled Asset Relief Program (TARP), was intended to prevent these companies from going bankrupt and causing further disruption to the economy. Amid the economic upheaval, the 2008 elections saw Democrat Barack Obama win the White House and the Democratic Party increase its majorities in both chambers of Congress.

The new president proposed an ambitious legislative agenda, which Pelosi and the House Democrats supported. In February 2009 Congress passed the American Recovery and Reinvestment Act (ARRA). A package of government spending increases and tax cuts, ARRA was intended to stimulate the foundering economy. But many Republicans objected to the price tag of approximately $800 billion, due to the sharp increase in budget deficits and the national debt.

Creating a system of universal health insurance had been a major Obama campaign promise, and the Democrats took up the issue early in the 111th Congress. In the House of Representatives, three committees held hearings throughout the spring, ultimately collaborating on a bill that was introduced in mid-July. Although no Republican representatives supported the bill, it passed the House in November.

The Senate, meanwhile, was working on its own health care reform legislation. Just as in the House, Senate Republicans were united in opposing the measure. In December, Democrats in the Senate overcame a Republican filibuster and passed, on a strict party-line vote, the Patient Protection and Affordable Care Act.

The House and Senate bills were similar, but there were a few important differences. To create the final law, the Senate and House would have to resolve these differences in a conference committee. Then both chambers would vote (without the ability to offer amendments) on the resulting bill, called a conference report.

Before that happened, however, Democrats were dealt a major blow. On January 19, 2010, Republican Scott Brown won a special election in Massachusetts to serve out the remainder of Ted Kennedy's Senate term (Kennedy had died the previous August). Now Democrats

President Obama signs an executive order related to the Patient Protection and Affordable Care Act. The legislation was the signature achievement of the Obama administration, but it angered many conservatives.

no longer had the 60 votes they needed to end a Republican filibuster, which could keep the legislation tied up in the Senate indefinitely.

Unless the House voted for the Senate bill, health care reform was dead. But many House Democrats objected to provisions in the Senate legislation. To win them over, Obama and Pelosi promised to address their concerns in another bill, which could be passed in the Senate through a controversial procedure known as reconciliation. Reconciliation bills—which involve budget-related matters—can't be filibustered, and the ability to offer amendments is limited.

Republicans were outraged at this tactic, but it succeeded. On March 21, 2010, the House approved the Patient Protection and Affordable Care Act that the Senate had passed, then effectively amended the bill by passing the Health Care and Education Reconciliation Act. After President Obama signed the former act into law, the Senate took up and passed the latter on March 25.

BACKLASH

Passage of the Patient Protection and Affordable Care Act satisfied a longtime goal of Democratic Party legislators. However, the bill and other programs of the Obama administration prompted a backlash from conservatives who were opposed to increased spending and the expansion of government. During 2009 and 2010 many of these protesters held angry rallies. They considered themselves patriots, just like the American colonists who had protested unfair British taxes before the Revolutionary War.

This "Tea Party" movement threw the 2010 midterm elections into chaos, as conservative candidates challenged more moderate Republicans in primary elections. When the dust settled, the Republicans had gained 63 seats in the House and regained control of the chamber. John Boehner of Ohio became Speaker when the 112th Congress convened in January 2011.

Boehner had a difficult challenge. Although the Republicans had a significant majority, the newly elected Tea Party candidates did not always agree with the "establishment" Republicans who had served in the House for many years. Meanwhile, the minority Democrats did all they could to block legislation that they opposed in the House. The 112th Congress would come to be considered one of the most politically polarized since the end of the Civil War, and also the least productive. It passed only 284 laws during its two-year session; historically, Congress passes 600 to 700 laws in each session.

Republicans maintained their majority in the 113th Congress (2013–2015), but the polarization continued. That Congress managed to pass 297 laws, the second-lowest total in American history. Many Americans were disgusted with the gridlock in Congress. The Gallup Poll reported in 2011 that only 19 percent of Americans approved of the job that Congress was doing. By 2014, even that low level of support had dropped to about 9 percent. Clearly, Congress needed to do something to regain the trust of the people it represents, but with the current situation of partisanship and gridlock, there seems to be no easy solution to this problem.

Chapter 5

The Size
of the House

In recent years, some political experts have come to believe that one way to reduce gridlock in Congress, as well as to improve its reputation with the American people, is to increase the number of members of the House of Representatives. Those who want to see Congress expand claim that there could be several benefits. They contend that a larger House would weaken each individual member's influence, which in theory would make it harder for lobbyists and special interest groups to influence legislation. They also note that smaller districts could reduce the amount of time that representatives have to spend campaigning, and give them more time to work on problems in Congress. And expanding the number of seats would enable the House to more accurately reflect the American population.

Changing the size of the House of Representatives would also have an effect on presidential elections. A presidential candidate who wins the popular vote in a state typically receives all of that state's electoral votes. The state's total Congressional representation determines the number of electoral votes it has. So Florida, with 27 members of the House and two senators, has a total of 29 electoral votes in the 2016 presidential election. North Dakota, with one representative and two senators, has three electoral votes. Expanding the House and reapportioning the seats would also lead to an expansion of the Electoral College. This matters because there have been times when a candidate has won a majority of the national vote, but not gained enough electoral votes to win the presidency. The most recent example occurred in the 2000 election, when Al Gore received over 540,000 more votes than George W. Bush, but Bush won 271 electoral votes to Gore's 266. If the House were larger, electoral votes could in theory be more fairly distributed among the states, making such an outcome less likely.

WHY 435 MEMBERS?

The U.S. Constitution gives Congress the authority to determine the number of members of the House of Representatives. Article 1, Section 2 of the Constitution set the size of Congressional districts at one representative for a minimum of 30,000 people, and it also allowed for larger districts as the population increased. The Constitution also says that every state must have at least one representative in the House.

During the first Congress, which was in session from 1789 to 1791, the House had 65 seats. Over the next 120 years, the size of the House varied during each two-year session. The admission of new states, as well as growth in the nation's population, affected the number of representatives in the House.

Throughout the nineteenth century, the number of House seats increased in almost every Congress, rising from 142 in the eighth Congress (1803–1805) to 238 in the 36th Congress (1859–1861). The number of Congressmen declined during the Civil War (1861–1865), as representatives from Southern states did not take seats in Congress. However, once the Southern states regained their Congressional representation in the 1870s, the number of House seats resumed their rise, reaching 386 in the 58th Congress (1903–1905). By the 63rd Congress (1913–1915), the House had grown to 435 seats. This figure was based on the 1910 Census, which reported the U.S. population at about 92 million people.

By this time, however, some experts were expressing concern that

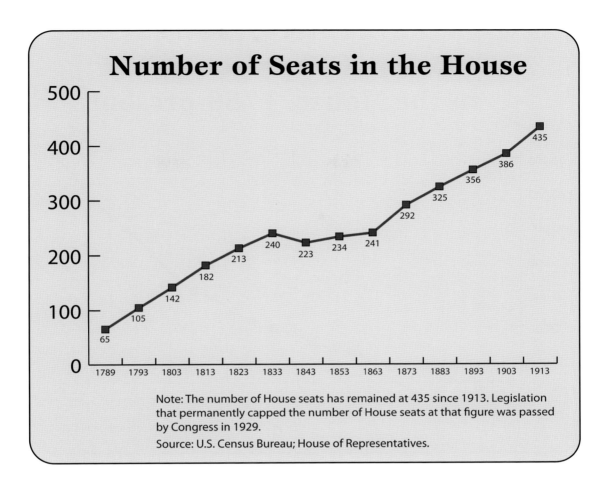

Number of Seats in the House

Note: The number of House seats has remained at 435 since 1913. Legislation that permanently capped the number of House seats at that figure was passed by Congress in 1929.

Source: U.S. Census Bureau; House of Representatives.

Congress would soon grow too large to continue to conduct its business in the Capitol building in Washington, D.C. There was also a belief that Congress could become too large to be able to function effectively as a lawmaking body.

After the 1920 Census, Congress did not add to or reapportion the seats in the House of Representatives. This was the first time that this had occurred in American history. Instead, in June 1929 Congress passed the Permanent Apportionment Act. This legislation capped the total number of representatives at the 435 total used since 1911. The Permanent Apportionment Act also set a formula for automatically reapportioning House seats after every census, so that the number of representatives from each state could change as the state's share of the

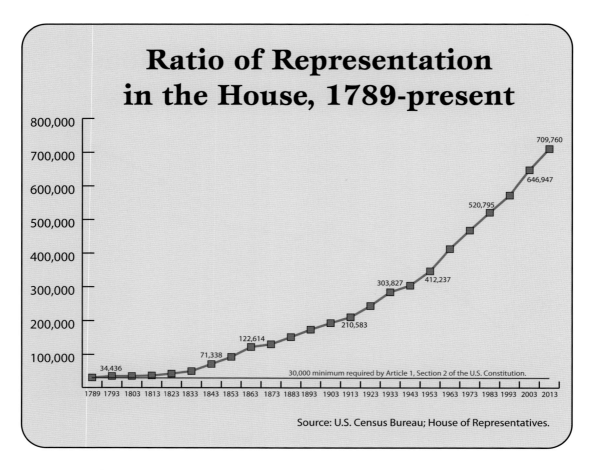

Ratio of Representation in the House, 1789–present

34,436

71,338

122,614

210,583

303,827

412,237

520,795

646,947

709,760

30,000 minimum required by Article 1, Section 2 of the U.S. Constitution.

Source: U.S. Census Bureau; House of Representatives.

national population changed. The formula was tweaked in 1941 to a more accurate method of allocating the seats based on population. That formula, known as the Huntington-Hill method, is still used today.

THE PROBLEMS WITH 435

The U.S. population has more than tripled over the past century, with the 2010 census recording a population of more than 309 million. In 1910, each House member represented about 210,000 people; in 2010, each House member represented more than 710,000 people. These figures are national averages, so some districts are considerably larger. Montana congressman Ryan Zinke, for example, represents more than a million Americans in the House of Representatives.

The size of congressional districts brings questions about whether one person can fairly represent the views and interests of more than 700,000 people. The original authors of the Constitution did not believe congressional districts should be too large. One of the first proposed amendments to the Constitution would have limited the size of congressional districts to 50,000 people. However, this amendment was not ratified by enough states and therefore never became part of the Constitution.

During the 1960s, a series of Supreme Court cases established the principle that all House delegations within a state should represent approximately the same number of people. The principle behind *Wesberry v. Sanders* (1964), *Reynolds v. Sims* (1964), and other rulings that were related to the creation of legislative district boundaries is "one person, one vote"—that in the United States, every citizen's vote should be given approximately equal weight. These rulings were orig-

Signs promote Congressional candidates outside a polling place in Virginia during the 2014 midterm election. In theory, less-populous House districts would make it easier for representatives to stay in touch with their constituents.

Counting People

During the Constitutional Convention in 1787, the delegates faced a challenging issue. The reason that the convention had been called was because many Americans were unhappy about the current system of government, known as the Articles of Confederation. This government included a national legislature in which every state was represented equally. This meant that a small state, such as Rhode Island, had just as much power in the legislature as a large state like Virginia did.

The delegates compromised by adopting a plan to divide the legislature into two bodies, the House of Representatives and the Senate. In the Senate, all of the states would be represented equally with two votes. But membership in the House of Representatives would be based on population. The states that had more people would have more representatives, and therefore more votes in the House.

This compromise raised a new question—should African-American slaves be represented in Congress? After all, slaves were considered to be property and did not have the same rights as free citizens. Delegates from the Southern states, where most of the slaves lived and worked, wanted slaves to be included in their population count. Doing that would give the Southern states more representatives in Congress. The Northern states did not want to include slaves as part of the state's population, so that the free citizens of the South would not be over-represented in the House. Ultimately, another compromise was reached. Article 1, Section 2 of the Constitution stated that slaves would be counted as three-fifths of a person for the purpose of determining seats in the House of Representatives.

Following the Civil War, the Thirteenth Amendment to the Constitution (1865) outlawed slavery, while the Fourteenth Amendment (1868) granted former slaves the full rights of citizenship in the United States. Since this time, all Americans have been counted as full persons for the purpose of determining Congressional representation.

inally issued to stop the widespread practice in the Southern states of gerrymandering, or drawing district boundaries in a way that squeezed African Americans into overcrowded districts in order to limit their representation in Congress.

Because of the way that state populations are concentrated into municipalities of various sizes, districts aren't expected to be exactly the same size, but they must be as close as reasonably possible. Thus Alabama's seven House districts in 2015 range from about 679,000 people to 706,500 people—a spread of about 27,500 from largest to smallest, or roughly 2 percent more or less than the average. New Jersey has 12 House districts, ranging from about 732,200 people to about 762,200. This is a spread of about 30,000 people, which again is about 2 percent from the average either way. When the districts in these states were drawn up after the 2010 census, the populations of the districts were within 1 percent.

Although districts within a state have to be roughly the same size, the size of congressional districts can vary greatly from state to state. Many people consider this one of the problems with the existing limit on the size of the House of Representatives.

Over-representation occurs when a state's ratio of representatives to population is lower than the average. In Alabama, the average district size is about 692,800, which makes it slightly lower than the national average of 710,000 per congressional district. Under-representation occurs when the state's ratio is higher than the average. In New Jersey, the average size of a House district in 2015 is about 745,000 people—just above the national average. However, both of these states are close enough to the national average that their ratio of representatives to population is pretty fair.

That is not always the case, however. The least populous state in the U.S., Wyoming, has one congressional district with a 2015 population of about 590,000. California, the most populous state, has 53 congressional districts that range in size from about 715,000 people to about 765,000 people. Thus a Congressperson from California represents more than 740,000 people on average, while a congressperson from Wyoming represents fewer than 600,000.

Here's another way to look at this. California's population is more than 66 times greater than Wyoming's. So for each Californian's vote to be equal to each Wyoming residents' vote in the House, the ratio of representatives should be 66 to 1. However, under the existing system of apportionment California has only 53 representatives in Congress to Wyoming's one.

For another example, the total population of Montana (1,023,579 in 2014) is just behind the population of Rhode Island (1,055,173). However, Rhode Island qualifies for two representatives in the House, meaning the state's average district size is about 527,000 people. As a result, Montana's single member of the House represents nearly twice as many people as each of Rhode Island's representatives.

PROPOSALS FOR CHANGE

Political scientists suggest that an increase in the size of the House, as well as a revision of the formula used for reapportionment of seats, is necessary to relieve the problems of over-representation and under-representation in the House.

One proposal is to expand the number of seats in the House so that the average ratio of representatives-to-population would be roughly equal to the smallest entitled congressional district. This plan is known as the Wyoming Rule, because Wyoming is currently the smallest state by population. If the Wyoming Rule were implemented today, it would set the target size of congressional districts at around 590,000, which would result in an increase in the number of seats from 435 to 545. The large states that are currently under-represented in Congress would all gain seats, with California adding 13 seats, Texas adding nine, New York adding seven, Florida adding six, and

Members of the House of Representatives are considerably wealthier than the people they represent. In 2013, according to the Center for Responsive Politics, the median net worth of a representative was over $1 million. The median net worth of all American households was $56,355.

Pennsylvania and Illinois each adding five. Other states would either gain seats or their apportionment would be unchanged.

However, the Wyoming Rule would not fully solve the issue of equal representation either. Under this plan Montana, which currently has the highest ratio of population to representation, would gain a second seat in the House, bringing its ratio into line with many other states. However, South Dakota would then become the most underrepresented state in the House, with a single district of more than 815,000 people.

In 2009, a lawsuit was filed against the government that challenged the current method of apportionment. The suit argued that the current system did not meet the "one person, one vote" standard set in the Constitution and supported by *Wesberry v. Sanders* and other court cases. However, the Supreme Court rejected this argument and dismissed the case in 2010. Despite this setback, today there are several organizations, such as Apportionment.US and 30000.org, that have continued to push for the expansion of the House of Representatives.

Glossary

apportionment—to distribute and allocate something, often according to a rule of proportional distribution.

bicameral—a legislative assembly that has two chambers or houses. The U.S. Congress includes the House of Representatives and the Senate.

bipartisan—referring to agreement or cooperation between two political parties that have opposing policies and ideological beliefs.

caucus—all the members of the Democratic or Republican Party in Congress, or a subset of them; a meeting of the members of a legislative body who are members of a particular political party, to select candidates or decide policy for that party.

civil rights—the personal liberties and legal rights that all individuals enjoy as citizens or residents of a country. For example, all residents of the United States have the right to express their opinions freely, to follow the religion of their choosing, to expect equal protection under the law, and to peacefully protest government policies with which they disagree. Those rights are guaranteed by the U.S. Constitution.

decennial—something that occurs every ten years.

deficit spending—when the federal government spends more than it takes in through taxes, and must borrow money to make up the difference in its annual budget.

gerrymander—to manipulate the boundaries of an electoral constituency so as to favor one party or class.

gridlock—a situation in which no progress or movement is possible.

incumbent—someone who already holds the office and is campaigning for reelection.

midterm election—in federal politics, the congressional election that is held two years after each presidential election.

national budget—a document specifying the amount of money the federal government expects to raise in taxes or acquire through loans and the amount of money the government plans to spend on its programs during the course of a year.

national debt—the amount of money the federal government owes.

over-representation—to be represented excessively, because the representative-to-population ratio is higher than the average.

polarization—a term referring to the situation in which two or more political parties have serious differences on political issues.

redistricting—to divide a geographic area into new political districts. With regard to the U.S. House of Representatives, redistricting occurs after each census to reflect population increases or decreases, as well as shifts of population within a state or the nation.

social welfare programs—government-run programs that are intended to protect citizens from unexpected problems or hardships. In the United States, such programs include Social Security, Medicare, and Medicaid, as well as Temporary Assistance for Needy Families (TANF), which is often referred to as "welfare."

special-interest group—an organized group that tries to influence the government into passing legislation that favor its interests.

under-representation—a situation in which the representative-to-population ratio for a political district is lower than the national average.

Further Reading

Adler, E. Scott, and John D. Wilkerson. *Congress and the Politics of Problem Solving*. New York: Cambridge University Press, 2013.

Bardes, Barbara, Mack Shelly, and Steffen Schmidt. *American Government and Politics Today: Essentials 2015-16 Edition*. Boston: Cengage Learning, 2015.

Curry, James M. *Legislating in the Dark: Information and Power in the House of Representatives*. Chicago: University of Chicago Press, 2015.

Draper, Robert. *When the Tea Party Came to Town: Inside the U.S. House of Representatives*. New York: Simon and Schuster, 2012.

Handlin, Amy. *Dirty Deals? An Encyclopedia of Lobbying, Political Influence, and Corruption*. Santa Barbara, Calif.: ABC-CLIO, 2014.

Hetherington, Marc J., and Thomas J. Rudolph. *Why Washington Won't Work: Polarization, Political Trust, and the Governing Crisis*. Chicago: University of Chicago Press, 2015.

Koger, Gregory. *Filibustering: A Political History of Obstruction in the House and Senate*. Chicago: University of Chicago Press, 2010.

La Raja, Raymond J. *Small Change: Money, Political Parties, and Campaign Finance Reform*. Ann Arbor: University of Michigan Press, 2008.

Mann, Thomas E., and Norman J. Ornstein. *It's Even Worse Than It Looks: How the American Constitutional System Collided with the New Politics of Extremism*. New York: Basic Books, 2013.

Spieler, Matthew. *The U.S. House of Representatives*. New York: Thomas Dunne Books, 2015.

Internet Resources

http://www.house.gov

The official website of the U.S. House of Representatives includes information about proceedings, bills being discussed, and House votes.

http://www.rollcall.com

The online version of *Roll Call*, a Washington, D.C.–based newspaper focusing on politics and policy.

https://www.democrats.org

Home page of the Democratic National Committee (DNC), an organization that provides leadership for the Democratic Party. The DNC coordinates national fundraising efforts and election strategy. It also develops and promotes the party platform—a list of its positions on various current issues.

https://www.gop.com

The home page of the Republican National Committee, which provides leadership for the party. It includes articles about Republican candidates, as well as the Republican position on current issues, known as the party platform.

Index

Numbers in **bold italic** refer to captions.

About the Author

Seth H. Pulditor is a longtime freelance editor. His other books include *Serial Killers* (Eldorado Ink, 2013), *Fascism* (Mason Crest, 2013), and biographies of football players DeSean Jackson and Drew Brees. A graduate of St. Joseph's University, he lives with his family near Philadelphia.